Soulwoman Circles
Life Planner 2016

Dr. Mia Rose
Karen Ferguson

soulwomancircles.com

Dr. Mia Rose
and
Karen Ferguson

Copyright © 2016 by Mia Rose and Karen Ferguson

All Rights Reserved

Cover and Interior Modifications by Ellie Searl, Publishista®

ISBN: 9780994514509

Soulwoman Publishing
Zilzie, Queensland, AU

Dedicated to YOU

Because You Deserve a Life that is
Beautiful,
Big-Hearted
and
Brilliant
Just Like You…

Meet the Team

Dr. Mia Rose and Karen Ferguson

Mia and Karen are founders of the Soulwoman Circles, a theme-based monthly online gathering for women to reconnect with their body and soul, align to the powerful cycles of the moon and the healing power of nature, and tune in to Spirit through guided intention setting, self-acceptance, self-love and supreme self-care.

Mia is an award-winning entrepreneur, author and psychologist, with over 25 years of experience working with private clients to transform the psychological factors, beliefs and emotions that sabotage their joy.

Karen joined the team in 2014 as Creative Director of the Soulwoman Circles and contributing Editor of Soulwoman eMagazine.

You can join the Soulwoman Circles at soulwomancircles.com.

Happy Days!

Are you ready to plan a life for yourself that has a positive, happy, soulful vibe? Are you hoping to make the most of each and every day? If so, this is the right Life Planner for you.

Every single day of your life is filled with opportunities for love, happiness, change, growth and celebration. Set an intention that from this day onwards, you will seize every opportunity you have to focus on the most inspirational and joyful aspects of your life. And then, let's make it so!

Your Life Planner is filled with empowering activities to help you move through this year with feelings of wonder, serenity and grace. May your 2016 be filled with 365 days that really matter!

How to Use your Life Planner

1. Create regular pockets of time for reflection in your Planner.
2. Gather a selection of your favourite pens.
3. Print out the pages you'd like to play with, or use your own journal.
4. Light a candle to create sacred space.
5. Put on some relaxing music.
6. Settle in with a sparkling water, glass of red, coffee, or herbal tea.
7. Put your feet up, and let go of all tension, self-judgement and expectations.
8. Be open to new discoveries.
9. Dream BIG.
10. Review your dreams regularly to keep on track.

TAKING STOCK

REFLECTIONS

Each and every year brings us gifts, lessons and blessings, but you have to consciously and actively seek them before they'll show up in all their glorious splendour to enrich your life.

No matter what month of the year it is right now, let's take a moment to reflect back on the past year of your life. Know that it showed up the way it did for a reason.

So let's celebrate and release the good, the bad and the ugly…
and clear the decks to make space for the miracles to come…

LAST YEAR'S THEME

Summarise the past year first in a word, then in a sentence, and lastly in a short paragraph.
Create an image to sum up the past year if you wish.

PLEASURE POWER

Describe some of the most pleasurable moments of
the past year in words or images.
What did pleasure look, sound, smell and taste like?
Most importantly, how did it FEEL?

WISHES AND DREAMS

Which of your wishes and dreams came true in the past year?
Reflect on what what you've accomplished and how you've grown.

MOST VALUABLE LESSONS

What were the disappointments and challenges you struggled with?
Look deep into those experiences and honour them.
What life lessons did you learn?

TRANSFORMATIONS

What did you discover about yourself in the past year? What were the transformations that occurred to make you MORE of who you really ARE?

UNFINISHED BUSINESS

Reflect on any unfinished tasks or unresolved issues.
What do you need to complete in order to move on?
What can you let go of?

BE DONE WITH IT

What do you need to rave or rant about, or express in words or images to feel that you've completed the past year? Do it.

GRATITUDE LIST

Write down the things that happened in the past year that you are most grateful for.

1.

2.

3.

4.

5.

6.

7.

8.

9.

10.

A Gratitude Practice

Let go of the past year with nothing but gratitude in your heart….

Light a candle to symbolise the past year.

Read each item on your Gratitude List out loud, beginning with the words, 'I'm grateful for…'

Inhale gratitude.

Exhale your gratitude out into the world.

Allow your feelings of gratitude to expand and grow until they fill every cell of your being.

Grab a pen and write a Love Note to the past year..

LOVE LETTER

The past year may not have been perfect, but it was a year of your life. Honour it, thank it for the gifts it brought into your life, bless it, and let it go...

Dear 2015....

LET'S CELEBRATE!

A celebration is in order, dear one! The past is over. It's done…

How will you celebrate?

WELCOMING IN 2016

TUNING IN…

Your Higher Self has all the answers to every question you could ever ask. Learn to tune in to your intuition.

There's a space of stillness in your inner being that holds all the answers to your most profound questions, including who you are and why you're here. It's the seat of your inner wisdom, the space where your Higher Self dwells.

The voice of your Higher Self sounds different than the voice of your mind. It has gentleness and clarity. If you consciously silence your mind chatter and ask questions in a space of stillness, the answers will come. Always.

Trust that even if you don't know, your Higher Self always knows. Dig deep. TRUST that you know.

CREATING THE DREAM

The single most important thing you can do to enjoy a spectacular year is to create the DREAM first. You have to set the stage for manifesting miracles.

Don't wait until you feel better to do this work. Don't wait until you have more time. You will never have the time until you make the time.

You can do this!

All you have to bring to the table is your WILLINGNESS to give it a go. All the guidance you need is right here... So tune in and start invoking your beautiful life right NOW!

2016 BIG DREAM

Go wild! Download your biggest, most beautiful dream to make this a fabulous year...

PICK A WORD

Isn't it wonderful how much possibility a new year holds? Every new year is a blank page to be filled with whatever you want. Let's choose a single word to guide you through the next 12 months. Pick a word that makes you feel inspired, encouraged and expanded.

Words are incredibly powerful portals through which magic can enter into your world. By choosing a sacred word, you're choosing what you want to manifest in your life.

Not sure what word is perfect for this very special year of your life? Do a bit of soul therapy by colouring in the design on the next page while playing with different words in your mind: Joy, Serenity, Focus, Transformation, Creativity? Love?

Which word FEELS the best? That's your winner!

Your Sacred Word for 2016

Allow your Word to be your North Star; a shining point of guidance that determines your direction and keeps you on track. And what do you do once you've chosen your Word? Well, playing with it is a good start…

- You can create a vision board for it.
- You can create a Pinterest board that represents it.
- You can meditate on it.
- You can write it on your bathroom mirror so you're reminded of it every morning.
- You can write it on a post-it note and stick it on your computer screen.
- You can collect objects that remind you of it.
- You can ask Auntie Google for quotes that include it.
- You can create affirmations that support your word.
- You can search for books on Amazon that include your word in the title.
- You can turn it into a #hashtag and use it on social media ~ often!

The Annual Forecast

Need a little guidance from the Universe?
Use your favourite tarot or oracle deck,
and draw three cards for the year to come.

Opportunities   Challenges   Outcome

LET'S PLAY!

What do you want the next year to FEEL like? Use words, colour and images to make your most heart-felt desires come alive.

BLISS LIST

What is on your bliss list – those warm fuzzies that make your soul sing? What sensory experiences fill your life with brilliance and light? What activities bring you the most joy?

Set an intention to do more of it!

YOU'RE ALLOWED…

What do you give yourself permission to do this year?

PROMISES TO KEEP

What needs to change for you to be happier in your own skin? What are the habits that no longer serve you? What new habits would you like to create? What promises are you making to yourself right now?

THE 'NO' LIST

It's so important to protect your precious energy and honour your values on a day-to-day basis. What will you no longer do or tolerate in your life?

Make the Law of Attraction Work for You

The Life Planner is designed as a tool to get positively aligned with your most beautiful dreams and desires. It's the perfect shortcut to send a clear and joyful message to the Universe about what you most want to create in your life.

Our intention is to help you harness the Law of Attraction by designing a big picture plan. It's also important to clarify the top actions you need to take so that you're not pulled in a thousand different directions.

By taking the time to be deliberate about what you want and how you want your year to play out, you'll set yourself up to fulfil your desires with perfect ease and flow.

So in case you're wondering how to make the Law of Attraction work for you, start here:

1. Decide what you want and be specific. Decide on the kind of year you want, the kind of month you want, and of course the day and the week and the hour. Decide the state of your body. Decide how you would like your relationships to play out. Decide what kind of environment you would like to live, work and play in.

2. Focus your thoughts and emotions on your desires.

3. Believe with absolute certainty that your dreams and desires will be fulfilled.

MANIFESTATIONS

What do you intend to manifest this year?

BLUEPRINTS

A Health Blueprint

Your body is truly amazing. It's made up of trillions of cells, each doing exactly what it was designed to do. If you tune in to the wisdom of your body, it will tell you exactly what you need to do to prevent dis-ease.

1. Treat your mind-body health as one of your most important responsibilities.
2. Know that good nutrition is the cornerstone of vibrant health. Keep your body hydrated. Eat intuitively, from a state of honouring your body's natural intelligence. It will tell you when you're hungry, what it needs for nourishment, and when you're full. Your body always knows.
3. Move and stretch your body as much as possible. Do yoga, tai chi, qi gong, or other slow-moving, soul-strengthening exercises. Walk, run, swim dance - whatever makes you feel alive!
4. Learn about natural remedies and therapies - and use them liberally to enhance your lifestyle.
5. Establish a good sleeping routine. Lack of sleep compromises immunity and limits your body's ability to repair itself.
6. Spend quiet time with yourself. Create pockets of time for indulgent self-care.
7. Supercharge your sex life and honour your ability to orgasm for a regular free flow of pleasurable energy.

HEALTH

What actions will you take to prioritise your health every day?

A Happiness Blueprint

Happiness isn't something that you have to create in your life. It already exists. Whether you tune into it, or not, is a daily choice.

1. Practice unconditional self-acceptance. Stop judging yourself or comparing yourself to others. Gain clarity about what you want and what inspires you.
2. Know that rich and satisfying relationships are the heart of true joy. Happiness is dependent on the nourishing connections you make.
3. Reboot your career. Don't be afraid to change what doesn't work for you. Do more of what you love.
4. Express yourself creatively. Sing. Dance. Paint. Draw. Doodle. Write… Do whatever makes your senses come alive.
5. Make giving more important than getting.
6. Be willing to forgive. Let go of hurts and disappointments. Don't hold grudges.
7. Set an intention to have fun every day. Nurture your sense of humour. You're never to old to play.
8. Spend time in nature. Feel the sun on your face. Hug trees. Walk barefoot on the grass.
9. Be mindful in everyday tasks. Remember that the point of power is always in the now.
10. Prioritise a daily spiritual practice. Read inspirational books. Meditate. Visualise the outcomes you want. Connect with your spirit guides. Pray.

HAPPINESS

What actions will you take to focus on your happiness every day?

An Abundance Blueprint

Abundance is about much more than the amount of money you have in the bank. You can be money-poor but wealthy in time, or joy, or blessings or serenity. Reflect on what abundance means to YOU.

1. Be aware of how your childhood conditioning impacted on your beliefs about abundance and wealth.
2. Honour what you do have. Know exactly what is flowing into your bank account and be clear on how you're spending it.
3. Actively recondition your mind to think wealth and prosperity thoughts.
4. Stop talking about what you don't want and what is not working. Put all your focus and energy on what you want to accomplish and what is going well.
5. Seek mentors. Follow the lead of those who have already created the kind of success you desire.
6. Love what you do. The Universe responds to the energy that you bring to Life.
7. Take consistent action in the direction of your dreams.8. Create space for abundance to flow in by getting rid of the clutter in your life. Make room for the new.
8. Share your good fortune. Don't wait until you're rich to share your blessings. The more you give, the more you will receive.
9. Practice gratitude. The more you are grateful for, the more will be given to you to be grateful for.

ABUNDANCE

What actions will you take to attract more abundance into your life every day?

MAKE IT HAPPEN

NEW MOON

The New Moon is the time in the moon cycle that signifies new beginnings. You will have new-found energy. It's a good time to start projects and pursue new opportunities.

WAXING MOON

The Waxing Moon is a growth phase, so it's the perfect time to work on your vision board. Focus on your life purpose, and what you hold dear. It's an appropriate time to begin a cleanse.

MOON MAGIC

WANING MOON

The waning moon is a great time to let go, forgive, and reflect on your goals and where you're at. This is the perfect time to meditate and spend time in solitude. Self-care is essential during this phase of the moon cycle.

FULL MOON

This is the most powerful time in the moon cycle, and you may be more sensitive and intuitive than usual. Surround yourself with like-minded souls and positive influences. This is a good time to rest, restore and flush toxins from your body.

90-DAY INTENTIONS
January - March

Break down your BIG dream into more manageable chunks. Consider creating a new vision board to put on your wall for this 90-day period to keep your intentions fresh in your mind.

JANUARY DREAM PAGES

Detox Your Life

Hello January!

January brings a feeling of renewal and blossoming growth. This is the month to get back on track after the festive season and rejuvenate your wellbeing.

Focus your attention this month on energising your entire life by releasing emotional, physical and energetic toxins.

January Intentions

New Moon: January 10
Full Moon: January 24

What steps can you take to detox your entire life?

TAKING ACTION!

What are the most important tasks you need to take action on to make progress this month?

The Monthly Forecast

Need a little guidance from the Universe?
Use your favourite tarot or oracle deck, and draw
three cards for January.

Opportunities　　　　　Challenges　　　　　Outcome

Crystal Power

Crystals are fascinating! They are both objects of beauty, and a beautiful way to simultaneously ground us and connect us to the divine.

We have chosen twelve crystals to focus on in our Life Planner - one for each month of the year. Keep in mind that all crystals can receive, store and amplify energy, and all can help you balance your body, mind, and spirit. It is our sincere hope that you will enjoy using your collection of crystals this year for healing, meditation, visualisation, divination and spiritual growth.

January: Red Jasper

This popular stone is excellent to help with quick thinking, increased confidence and getting results. It can also help you with courage if you need it.

To energise yourself with the red fire of courage, close your eyes and hold your red jasper stone between both palms of your hands, as if clasping them together in prayer. Imagine the stone slowly warming up your hands, and imagine the warmth spread and circulate through your entire body.

Think of one thing you want to do this month, something you've never done before, and perhaps thought you were incapable of doing. Imagine yourself taking action on it. Imagine the great results achieved.

End your visualisation with a few deep breaths, and remind yourself that anything is possible if you put your mind to it.

You are stronger and braver than you think!

GRATITUDE LIST
What are you most grateful for this month?

1.
2.
3.
4.
5.
6.
7.
8.
9.
10.

How to Do a Mandala Meditation

Mandalas are symbols of wholeness, harmony and ultimate perfection. A mandala meditation helps you to clear your mind and focus inward.

Here are the steps:

1. Make yourself comfortable in a quiet room, and place the mandala at eye level about an arm's length, or slightly more, in front of you.
2. Straighten your back and rest your hands in your lap, fingers laced together and palms uppermost.
3. Relax your eye muscles and focus on the mandala with a soft gaze. Blink only as often as necessary.
4. Do not be distracted by any thoughts that arise. If your attention wanders, bring it back each time to the mandala.
5. To begin with, practice for five minutes each day. As you become used to this form of meditation, extend your meditation practice to a full 20 or 30 minutes at each session.

Mandala Meditation

Interpretation

1. During your meditation, consider the dominant colours in this mandala. Pink is traditionally a feminine colour, and associated with the physical body. In mandalas, pink often reveals the pleasures and pain of life. The colour turquoise takes its name from the gemstone, and is often used in healing. There are also accents of orange and yellow to add warmth and light to this mandala. What other feelings are evoked when you look at the colours in this design?

2. The hearts in this mandala symbolise love - and perhaps the need to heal your heart. The heart may also symbolise a spiritual quest. Also think about other heart references in our language. We encourage people to take heart, or we may say that someone's heart is either broken with sadness or bursting with joy. What is true for you?

3. The dominant number in this mandala is eight, which is the number of stability, harmony and rebirth. This number also represents the sign for infinity, and can indicate the limitless spiralling movement of the cosmos. Isn't it beautiful?

Soul Therapy

REFLECTIONS

What went well this month? What didn't go so well? What would you like to do differently next month?

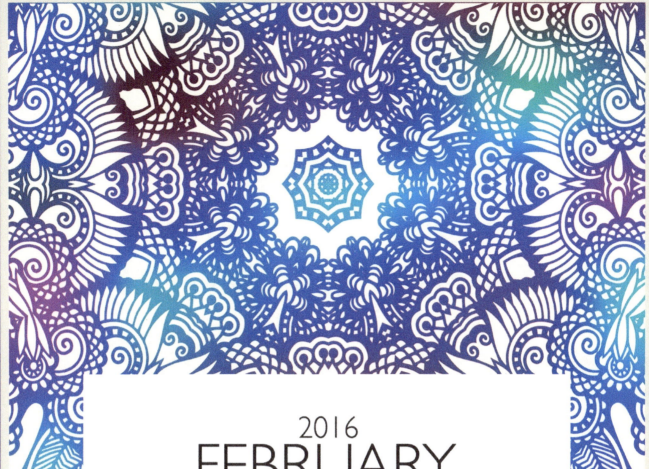

2016
FEBRUARY

Sun	Mon	Tue	Wed	Thu	Fri	Sat
	1	2	3	4	5	6
7	8	9	10	11	12	13
14	15	16	17	18	19	20
21	22	23	24	25	26	27
28	29					

JANUARY

MARCH

FEBRUARY DREAM PAGES

Luminous Self-Love

Hello February!

This is the month to release the layers of self-judgment and self-imposed expectations that make you feel trapped in a painful cycle of 'not-enoughness'.

We'd love for you to focus on celebrating yourself for the gorgeous, creative, vibrant goddess you truly are.

February Intentions

New Moon: February 9
Full Moon: February 23

How do you intend to practice luminous self-love this month?

TAKING ACTION!

What are the most important tasks you need to take action on to make progress this month?

The Monthly Forecast

Need a little guidance from the Universe?
Use your favourite tarot or oracle deck, and draw
three cards for February.

Opportunities					Challenges					Outcome

February: Carnelian

Orange carnelian is a wonderful stone to enhance your motivation, endurance and sense of adventure. It is also associated with eloquence and self-confidence.

Carnelian was traditionally sacred to Isis, the Egyptian goddess who revived her dead husband, and for that reason, carnelian now symbolises all faithful wives and companions.

To work with carnelian, imagine that you ARE this gorgeous crystal. Relax, slow your breathing, and picture yourself glowing in brilliant orange hues. Notice how intense and alive it feels to tap into the power of orange.

Know that you have the ability, resources and confidence to conquer all challenges.

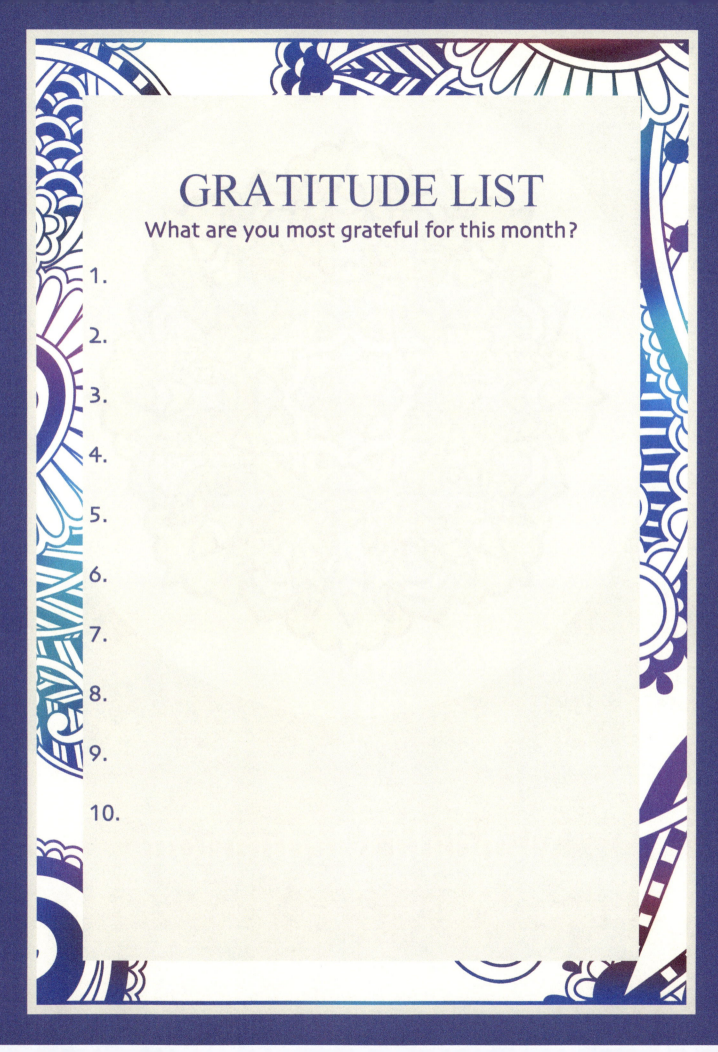

GRATITUDE LIST
What are you most grateful for this month?

1.
2.
3.
4.
5.
6.
7.
8.
9.
10.

Mandala Meditation

Interpretation

1. During your meditation, consider the dominant colours in this mandala. Green is the colour of nature, and it reminds us of growing things and fresh scents. Pink often reveals the pleasures and pain of life, and turquoise is often used in healing. There are also accents of orange and yellow for a touch of warmth.

2. The green leaves in this mandala symbolise spring and the renewal of life. The pink star in the middle symbolises heavenly favour and guidance. According to the Greek philosophers stars are related to the soul. The soul star generates our inspirations, creativity and enthusiasm. What is the state of your soul star right now?

3. The dominant numbers here are one, eight, and sixteen. One (the star) is symbolic of a new beginning or the initiation of a process, like the single acorn with which a tree begins. Eight is the number of stability, harmony and rebirth. And sixteen is of course two times eight, and so strengthening the message of eight. How is any of this applicable to your life right now?

Soul Therapy

REFLECTIONS

What went well this month? What didn't go so well? What would you like to do differently next month?

MARCH DREAM PAGES

Vibrational Mastery

Hello March!

In order to access a higher state of frequency to fulfil your heart's desires, you need to show commitment to the way you're living your life.

This month, the focus is on connecting with the Source of All Creation to raise your energetic vibration for manifestation and healing purposes.

March Intentions

New Moon: March 9
Full Moon: March 23

How do you intent to raise your energetic vibrations this month?

TAKING ACTION!

What are the most important tasks you need to take action on to make progress this month?

The Monthly Forecast

Need a little guidance from the Universe?
Use your favourite tarot or oracle deck, and draw
three cards for March.

Opportunities   Challenges   Outcome

March: Yellow Jade

Yellow jade is associated with the radiance and optimism of the sun. It is cheerful and energetic, and known to be a stone of assimilation and discrimination.

Yellow jade protects against negative energy and brings hope. It can also assist in healing family issues.

Here's how to do a simple protection ritual: Hold the stone in your hand and breathe deeply. As you become calm and focused, imagine that a golden light begins to emanate from the crystal's very core. Allow it to grow in your mind's eye until it's big enough to create a huge bubble of protective light around you.

Stay within the warm yellow glow for a few minutes, visualising a feeling of warmth and safety. Know that you are completely protected from
all possible harm.

Whenever you enter a challenging environment, hold your crystal in your hand to restore a feeling of safety security.

GRATITUDE LIST
What are you most grateful for this month?

1.
2.
3.
4.
5.
6.
7.
8.
9.
10.

Mandala Meditation

Interpretation

1. Appreciate the different shapes of this mandala, starting with the star in the middle that depicts the divine source of all life, pulsing with energy.

2. Let your eyes rest on the colours. Let all the energies of the mandala float deeper and deeper into your inner being, until your mind achieves a perfect and peaceful resonance.

3. The dominant number in this mandala is eight, also symbolising the Buddha's Eightfold Path: right speech, right action, right livelihood, right effort, right mindfulness, right concentration, right view and right thought.

4. Look at the turquoise shapes on the rim of the mandala, and ask yourself: What in your life needs healing right now? Absorb the mandala into yourself as a guide and commitment to purity and wholeness.

Soul Therapy

REFLECTIONS

What went well this month? What didn't go so well?
What would you like to do differently next month?

90-DAY INTENTIONS
April - June

Break down your BIG dream into more manageable chunks. Consider creating a new vision board to put on your wall for this 90-day period to keep your intentions fresh in your mind.

APRIL DREAM PAGES

Prosperity Programming

Hello April!

Now is the time to redefine what you want to get out of life and what you want to give in return. Let's focus our efforts this month on letting go of scarcity beliefs and stepping into abundance in a big, beautiful way!

April Intentions

New Moon: April 7
Full Moon: April 22

What steps can you take to increase your prosperity from here on?

TAKING ACTION!

What are the most important tasks you need to take action on to make progress this month?

The Monthly Forecast

Need a little guidance from the Universe?
Use your favourite tarot or oracle deck, and draw three cards for April.

Opportunities   Challenges   Outcome

April: Aventurine

Aventurine, with its soothing green colour and glistening sheen, is one of the loveliest crystals. It's a handy stone to have when you undertake any creative adventure. Aventurine is a holistic, all-purpose healer, and green stones in general promote material and financial success.

Take an aventurine stone and hold it in the palm of your hand. Imagine all the money in the world flowing to you through the power of the crystal that you're holding in your hand. Then imagine it all flowing away into the Universe, and back to you again.

Reflect on money as a free flow of energy, and how much abundance you already have in your life. Give thanks for all you own, and all you have available to give and share.

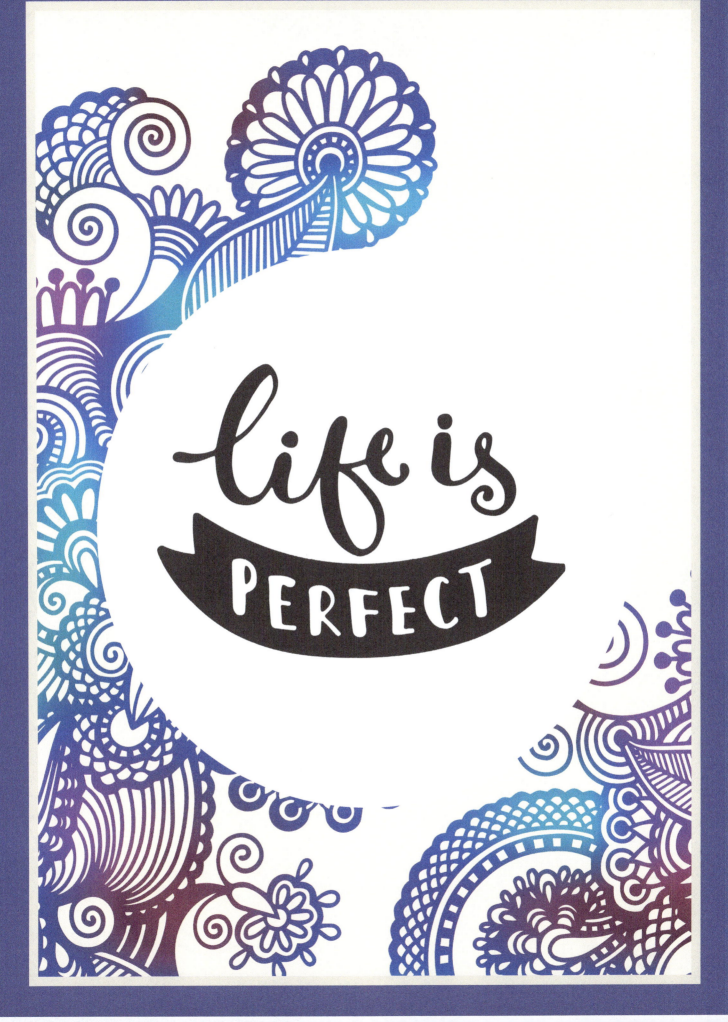

GRATITUDE LIST
What are you most grateful this month?

1.
2.
3.
4.
5.
6.
7.
8.
9.
10.

Mandala Meditation

Interpretation

1. This mandala starts with a tiny blue flower in the center, and then flows outwards towards the rim of the circle in shades of pink and purple bell-shaped flowers. The pink in this mandala directs you to ask what is in need of protection in your life right now. Purple, the colour of royalty, carries the suggestion of sacrifice and personal dedication to spirituality. The blue at the edges appear as a special expression of feminine attributes such as compassion, devotion, loyalty and unfailing love. White suggests purity, virginity, and spirituality. What resonates with you right now?

2. The flowers in this mandala may signify the quickening of your personal and spiritual growth cycle. They may also signal the fulfilling of a goal or task which has taken much dedication on your part. What else is blooming in your life?

3. The dominant number in this mandala is eight, considered by Jung as a symbol of wholeness because it is a multiple of the number four, a preeminent symbol of the Self. What do you need to explore in yourself right now? What is there to learn?

Soul Therapy

REFLECTIONS

What went well this month? What didn't go so well?
What would you like to do differently next month?

2016
MAY

Sun	Mon	Tue	Wed	Thu	Fri	Sat
1	2	3	4	5	6	7
8	9	10	11	12	13	14
15	16	17	18	19	20	21
22	23	24	25	26	27	28
29	30	31				

APRIL

JUNE

MAY DREAM PAGES

Health, Healing & Harmony

Hello May!

Let's increase our efforts to live a nutrient-rich life that will heal us – body, mind and soul. More than ever before, it's important to reconnect your life to a more holistic lifestyle to establish balance in every aspect of your life.

May Intentions

New Moon: May 7
Full Moon: May 22

What steps will you take to improve your health this month?

TAKING ACTION!

What are the most important tasks you need to take action on to make progress this month?

The Monthly Forecast

Need a little guidance from the Universe?
Use your favourite tarot or oracle deck, and draw
three cards for May.

Opportunities　　　　　Challenges　　　　　Outcome

May: Sodalite

Sodalite, also known as the student's stone, is a dark blue stone with white bands. Its crisp colour is clean and refreshing.

Brilliant sodalite can help you concentrate, remember, learn and organise your knowledge. Some people keep sodalite near their computers and television sets to absorb electromagnetic emissions.

Use sodalite to help you generate sweet dreams. Put a small sodalite crystal under your pillow, or a larger one under your bed.

For lucid dreams, you may want to experiment with taping the crystal to your third-eye chakra in the middle of your forehead. Try, if you can, to be aware of the crystal even as you sleep, to remind you to take control of the course of events and make decisions in your dreams.

GRATITUDE LIST
What are you most grateful for this month?

1.
2.
3.
4.
5.
6.
7.
8.
9.
10.

Mandala Meditation

Interpretation

1. Orange and teal are such a beautiful combination! The orange in this mandala, traditionally the hue of fertility, love and splendour, generates upbeat, happy emotions. Orange also reminds of the energy of the sun which drives your earthly being. The teal has calming and harmonising qualities to help relieve anxiety and stress.

2. Nature is a source of inspiration for this mandala with its stunning eight-petalled flower. Flowers are symbols of our impermanence. They also remind us of the inner beauty that flourishes if we conduct ourselves well in thought and deed.

3. Turn your attention to the heart of this mandala and meditate on a journey into yourself. Feel into how you relate to the flowering of spirituality within yourself.

3. Whilst contemplating this mandala, ask yourself if you have any unresolved issues that deal with love, self-esteem or relationships with others. If you do, what can you do to find resolution?

Soul Therapy

REFLECTIONS

What went well this month? What didn't go so well? What would you like to do differently next month?

JUNE DREAM PAGES

The Spiritual Kitchen

Hello June!

There is an amazing link between spiritual awakening and nourishment, and this is the perfect month to explore what you are really hungry for.

Let's experiment with self-regulation, cook up some magic, and explore the mystic alchemy of food.

June Intentions

New Moon: June 5
Full Moon: June 20

How can you nourish yourself spiritually with food this month?

TAKING ACTION!

What are the most important tasks you need to take action on to make progress this month?

The Monthly Forecast

Need a little guidance from the Universe?
Use your favourite tarot or oracle deck, and draw three cards for June.

Opportunities					Challenges					Outcome

June: Amethyst

Amethysts are regal, violet-coloured stone. Their soothing sense of energy gives your intuition a boost.

Choose an amethyst to work with and place it on the palm of your hand. Close your eyes and imagine the colour purple as a stream of light above your head. Keep holding the vision of the purple light stream as you imagine it moving down slowly to shower you in its beautiful purple light.

Visualise the colour purple filling you with a sense of universal connection and a feeling of utter peace.

Bask in the colour purple for a little while, and when you're ready to end your visualisation, look at the crystal in your hand and affirm: 'I am filled with the light of the Universe.'

Place the crystal under your pillow to enhance your spiritual awareness.

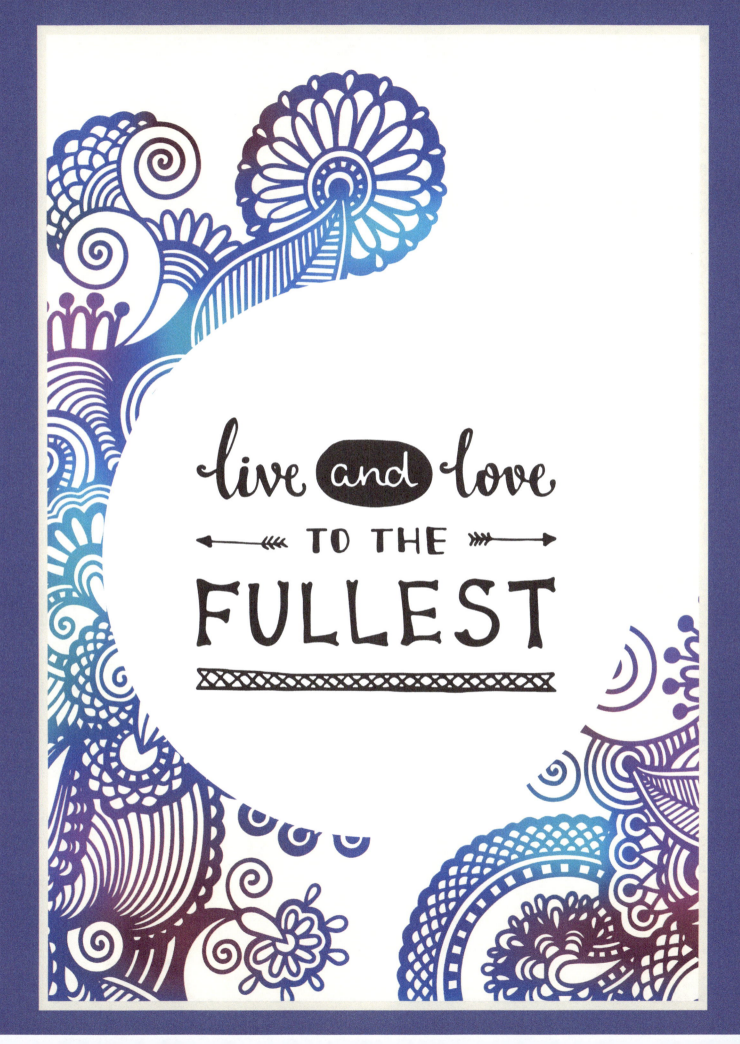

GRATITUDE LIST
What are you most grateful for this month?

1.
2.
3.
4.
5.
6.
7.
8.
9.
10.

Mandala Meditation

Interpretation

1. This mandala, with its eight pink hearts stimulate feelings of compassion and loving-kindness. Focus on the pink star in the center of the mandala, and open your heart to unconditional love and acceptance for yourself and others.

2. Now rest your eyes on the intermingling shapes and colours that surround the central star. Feel the blooming of compassion inside yourself, like a beautiful warm glow.

3. Let your eyes drift to the yellow and green petals of the flower and meditate on the healing that takes place when compassion's seeds fall on fertile soil.

4. As you contemplate this intricate design, ask yourself if there is anyone in your life that you need to forgive in order to find healing for your own heart. Consider if there is something you need to forgive yourself for.

5. Send loving-kindness out into the world from a heart filled with love.

Soul Therapy

REFLECTIONS

What went well this month? What didn't go so well? What would you like to do differently next month?

90-DAY INTENTIONS
July – September

Break down your BIG dream into more manageable chunks. Consider creating a new vision board to put on your wall for this 90-day period to keep your intentions fresh in your mind.

JULY DREAM PAGES

The Art of Simplicity

Hello July!

Embracing simplicity is the key to reclaim your peace of mind. Simplicity helps to banish busyness, confusion and complexity from your life.

This month, we encourage you to celebrate the luxury of less. Let go of your attachment to 'stuff', and get serious about de-cluttering your home, office and mindset.

July Intentions

New Moon: July 4
Full Moon: July 20

How can you embrace the luxury of less this month?

TAKING ACTION!

What are the most important tasks you need to take action on to make progress this month?

The Monthly Forecast

Need a little guidance from the Universe?
Use your favourite tarot or oracle deck, and draw
three cards for July.

Opportunities	Challenges	Outcome

July: Clear Quartz

Quartz is a common mineral in the earth's crust and quartz crystals are readily available to add to your collection of stones. Clear quartz is arguably the most versatile crystal. You can use it for any metaphysical purpose, including meditation, divination, dream work, and healing.

Clear quartz makes a good, all-purpose elixir. Clean it thoroughly with a wet washcloth and a little dish soap, then rinse well. Put your crystal in a plain glass jar with no labels. Fill the jar with purified, spring or distilled water, and cover the top of the jar with a clean piece of cloth.

Put the jar out in the sun for two to four hours, or leave it out overnight in the light of the moon. Once your elixir has absorbed the power of the crystal in conjunction with the energy of the sun or moon, add an ounce of brandy to stabilise and preserve it. Seal in a glass container and store in the pantry or fridge.

Don't drink the elixir straight… when you're ready to use it, simply add a drop or two to a glass of regular drinking water. You can also add a drop to your perfume.

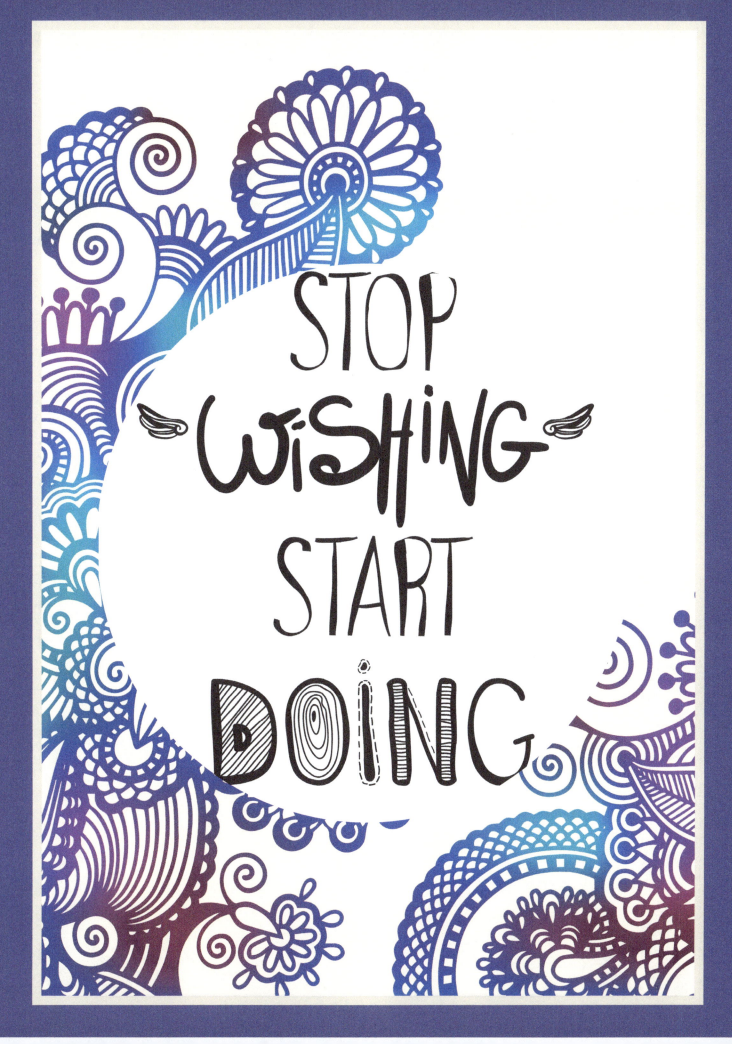

GRATITUDE LIST
What are you most grateful for this month?

1.
2.
3.
4.
5.
6.
7.
8.
9.
10.

Mandala Meditation

Interpretation

1. Gaze at the flower at the central heart of the mandala. Feel yourself relaxing as you contemplate the gradual blossoming of a state of peace in your inner being.

2. The dominant number in this mandala is seven, which is an important number in the mysticism of the ancients. Seven colours were identified in the rainbow, which was believed to be a bridge for the gods to earth. Each god was given his own day, and the seven-day week was established to mark time.

3. In ancient literature, the number seven denotes the completion of a cycle of time. Whilst meditating on this mandala, ask yourself if there are any cycles in your own life that are coming to an end, as well as what you need to let go of in order to move into new beginnings. You may also want to focus on the natural rhythms of time, and honour them with the reverent consideration of our ancestors for whom every day of the week was holy.

3. Finally, take in the perfect symmetry of the mandala's design, and feel yourself effortlessly relaxing into a state of healing and bliss.

Soul Therapy

REFLECTIONS

What went well this month? What didn't go so well? What would you like to do differently next month?

2016
AUGUST

Sun	Mon	Tue	Wed	Thu	Fri	Sat
	1	2	3	4	5	6
7	8	9	10	11	12	13
14	15	16	17	18	19	20
21	22	23	24	25	26	27
28	29	30	31			

JULY

SEPTEMBER

AUGUST DREAM PAGES

The Wild Feminine

Hello August!

When you truly embody your feminine essence, your whole life is transformed. You become grounded, sensual and positively radiant.

This month, we encourage you to explore your sacred essence and express your personal power so that you can experience more passion and fulfilment in your life.

August Intentions

New Moon: August 3
Full Moon: August 18

How will you express your wild feminine power this month?

TAKING ACTION!

What are the most important tasks you need to take action on to make progress this month?

The Monthly Forecast

Need a little guidance from the Universe?
Use your favourite tarot or oracle deck, and draw
three cards for August.

Opportunities	Challenges	Outcome

August: Howlite

Howlite is a silky, snowy white stone with marble-like veins of gray or black. It's a pleasing crystal to touch, because it feels like smooth, cool porcelain.

Howlite has a lovely, calming energy and can be used to relieve anxiety and tension. It also soothes intense emotions. Howlite calms racing thoughts and help you to relax in preparation for meditation or sleep. For a good night's rest, place this beautiful stone under your pillow.

Howlite helps to calm unreasonable anger, either your own or anger that is directed at you.

Carry a piece with you in your pocket to shield you against rage and promote calm communication.
Hold it whenever you enter into a hostile environment to empower you with its protective energy.

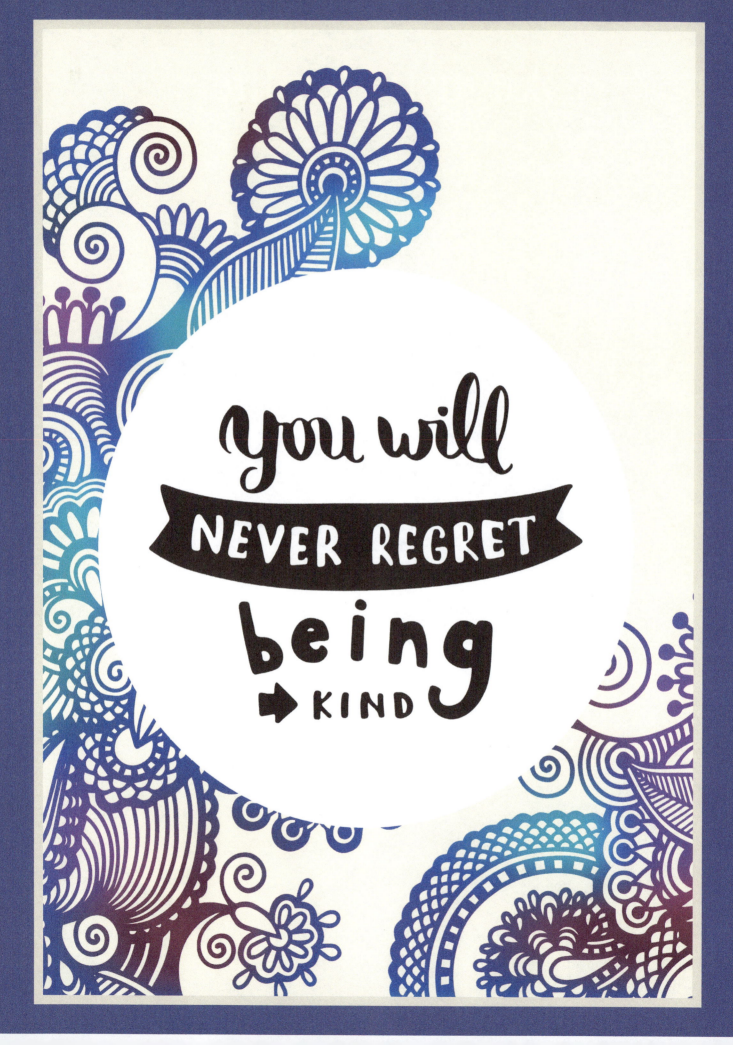

GRATITUDE LIST
What are you most grateful for this month?

1.
2.
3.
4.
5.
6.
7.
8.
9.
10.

Mandala Meditation

Interpretation

1. The dominant number in this intricate design is twelve, which is symbolic of cosmic order. Twelve corresponds to the signs in the zodiac, and the number of months in the year. Twelve suggests completion, wholeness and spiritual growth.

2. Gaze at the vibrant colours in this mandala whilst contemplating how we are all children of the cosmos. We are all one - and beautiful in our diversity. Remind yourself to expand your horizons from your own individual concerns by looking outward to the vast, awe-inspiring Universe. The immensity of the Universe is a part of yourself, and the cosmos is very much your home. Reflect on how you are connected to all other people by a powerful bond of spirit.

3. Finally, bathe your senses in the dynamic energy of the mandala's vivid beauty. Feel its energy deep inside your soul. Have no fear. Know that you are safe to express all the dynamic, complex aspects of your true, authentic nature. Life is beautiful. All is well.

Soul Therapy

REFLECTIONS

What went well this month? What didn't go so well? What would you like to do differently next month?

2016
SEPTEMBER

Sun	Mon	Tue	Wed	Thu	Fri	Sat
				1	2	3
4	5	6	7	8	9	10
11	12	13	14	15	16	17
18	19	20	21	22	23	24
25	26	27	28	29	30	

AUGUST

OCTOBER

SEPTEMBER DREAM PAGES

Nature's Prescriptions
Hello September!

Get your glow on as you explore a world of wellness with natural recipes for your household.

We encourage you to build your own personal apothecary of essential oils, and to make the simple scents and pleasures of aromatherapy a normal part of your everyday life.

September Intentions

New Moon: September 1
Full Moon: September 17

What can you do to embrace nature's prescriptions this month?

TAKING ACTION!

What are the most important tasks you need to take action on to make progress this month?

The Monthly Forecast

Need a little guidance from the Universe?
Use your favourite tarot or oracle deck, and draw
three cards for September.

Opportunities   Challenges   Outcome

September: Rose Quartz

Rose quartz is the stone of peace and emotional healing. It's also a romantic stone - its rosy colour is associated with all forms of love and friendship.

Rose quartz is a spectacular choice to aid you in taking a healing bath.

Run the bath as you normally would but add relaxing essential oils like lavender or chamomile. Consider indulging yourself with a few floating petals. Roll up a towel to put under your head, and light a candle or two.

Line your rose quartz crystals up on the side of the tub so you can bring them into the water with you.

And…. relax…

If you're worried that your crystals could go down the drain, tie them up in a piece of cloth or slip them into a mesh bag. Their energy will still be able to flow into your bathwater.

After your bath, place your crystals by your bed to receive their loving energy.

GRATITUDE LIST
What are you most grateful for this month?

1.
2.
3.
4.
5.
6.
7.
8.
9.
10.

Mandala Meditation

Interpretation

1. This dazzling mandala reminds of the warm glow of the rising or setting sun. Reflect on how the sun is unimaginably distant yet directly controls the seasons. As the source of heat, all physical energy comes from the sun. As the source of all light, ithe sun represents vitality, passion, courage and truth.

2. Consider the impact of the palette of colours in this mandala on your emotions and mood. Note that orange is linked with the sacral chakra and used to stimulate creativity, positivity and sexual energy. The yellow at the edge of the mandala aligns with the solar plexus chakra, which governs energy, drive and motivation. Do you feel in need of healing in either of these areas in your own life?

3. Looking deep into yourself, contemplate your greatest riches: your vitality, vibrancy and warmth. Reflect on your ability to shine brightly despite the darkness in the world. Think of yourself as looking right into the depths of your true, authentic nature. You are unique and beautiful, and the deeper you penetrate the layers of your being, the brighter you shine.

Soul Therapy

REFLECTIONS

What went well this month? What didn't go so well? What would you like to do differently next month?

90-DAY INTENTIONS
October - December

Break down your BIG dream into more manageable chunks. Consider creating a new vision board to put on your wall for this 90-day period to keep your intentions fresh in your mind.

OCTOBER DREAM PAGES

A Journey in Joy

Hello October!

Go beyond positive thinking and step into a genuine sense of happiness that aligns with your spiritual expansion.

We encourage you to tap into the deeper self this month. You will gain immeasurable joy from living a purposeful life filled with love, contribution and meaning.

October Intentions

New Moon: October 1
Full Moon: November 14
New Moon: October 31

How will you embrace the feeling of joy this month?

TAKING ACTION!

What are the most important tasks you need to take action on to make progress this month?

The Monthly Forecast

Need a little guidance from the Universe?
Use your favourite tarot or oracle deck, and draw
three cards for October.

Opportunities					Challenges					Outcome

October: Tiger's Eye

Tiger's eye is a brown chalcedony with gold highlights. When tiger's eye is cut and polished, it reveals a narrow band of brilliant light that looks like the eye of a tiger.

Ancient Romans carried tiger's eye into battle, believing that it would speed up their reaction time. Today, tiger's eye is used to enhance determination to pursue your dreams with patience and tenacity.

Tiger's eye can also be used to bring more abundance into your life. Take a piece of tiger's eye outside on a cloudless evening, place it in the palm of your hand and hold it up to the moonlight for a minute or two.

Repeat the following petition:

'Bless this crystal with manifesting powers, so that what I need for myself and others will arrive in perfect time for the good of All.'

GRATITUDE LIST
What are you most grateful for this month?

1.
2.
3.
4.
5.
6.
7.
8.
9.
10.

Mandala Meditation

Interpretation

1. The beauty of the lotus at the heart of this mandala is that it remains untouched by the water or mud that nourishes it. The lotus denotes pure spirit. As we flower spiritually, love and compassion flow from our hearts into the world - tender as the lotus petals and strong as the life force itself. Enter the lotus in your meditation and allow the lotus to enter you.

2. Turn your attention to the flower as a whole. Take its six petalled radiance into your mind and heart. Six is the number of creativity, perfection and equilibrium. Six in a mandala can also signify the achievement of goals, and a deepening sense of spirituality. Notice the candles burning at the heart of each petal and consider how brightly your own light is shining in the world.

3. In the circle of this mandala, we experience perfect unity and completeness. Feel yourself effortlessly relax into a state of healing symmetry.

Soul Therapy

REFLECTIONS

What went well this month? What didn't go so well? What would you like to do differently next month?

NOVEMBER DREAM PAGES

The Magic of Mindfulness

Hello November!

Mindfulness allows you to rediscover your spiritual roots and develop a deeper sense of self-awareness and connection to your unique purpose.

We encourage you to consciously practice mindfulness every day. You may also want to step up your breath-work and meditation practices to help you feel more energised and alive!

November Intentions

Full Moon: November 14
New Moon: November 29

What can you do to be more mindful in all you do this month?

TAKING ACTION!

What are the most important tasks you need to take action on to make progress this month?

The Monthly Forecast

Need a little guidance from the Universe?
Use your favourite tarot or oracle deck, and draw
three cards for November.

Opportunities   Challenges   Outcome

November: Obsidian

Obsidian is a rich, black volcanic glass, and arguably the most grounding and protective stone available.

Black is an important energy in the crystal kingdom and black stones are often used as stones of prophecy. On another level, they symbolise self-control and resilience.

To work with obsidian, light a candle and place it on a table in front of you. Concentrate for a while on the stone, visualising yourself entering into the stone's very being. Imagine sinking deeper into the darkness until you find a source of brilliant light.

As you focus on the eternal light within the dark, be aware of a calm and restful silence. Imagine the mysteries of the Universe unfolding within you.

Relax into the stillness until you're ready to end your visualisation.

Then touch the stone with both hands to ground you in reality.

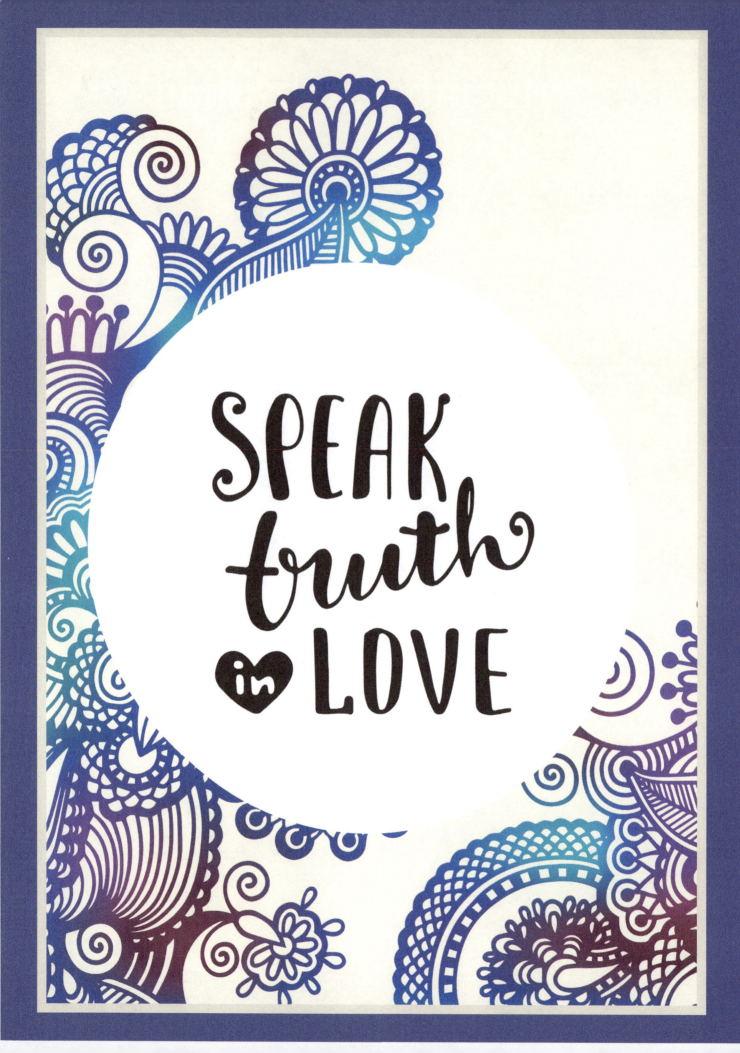

GRATITUDE LIST
What are you most grateful for this month?

1.

2.

3.

4.

5.

6.

7.

8.

9.

10.

Mandala Meditation

Interpretation

1. The dominant numbers in this mandala are four, eight and sixteen. Four suggests balance, wholeness and completion. Four also sets boundaries and defines limits. We orient ourselves according to the four directions and honour the four elements (earth, air, fire and water). In mandalas, patterns of four often expand into patterns of eight and sixteen, revealing a strong influence of the archetype of the Self.

2. Rest your gaze on the eight eyes in this mandala. The eye is associated with the ability to see both literally and metaphorically. Contemplate your own 'third eye', which is positioned between the brows, and symbolises the divine. The message of the eyes is to pay close attention to what you see - and also perhaps to what you don't want to see.

3. The eight small spirals in the orange section depict the orderly movement that occurs in the universe and a growth towards wholeness. Consider whether you are feeling in tune with cosmic rhythms; whether you are in flow or perhaps resisting the natural flow of life.

3. Rest your eyes on the small stars in the midnight blue section of the mandala. Stars glitter in the night sky and guide the wanderer home. Ancients considered stars symbols of heavenly favour and guidance. Stars are also related to the soul.

Soul Therapy

REFLECTIONS

What went well this month? What didn't go so well? What would you like to do differently next month?

DECEMBER DREAM PAGES

Rhythms of the Earth

Hello December!

This month, we encourage you to cultivate a conscious connection with Mother Nature.

Get back in touch, back in your body, and back down to earth. Breathe deeply. Seek serenity, joy and inner peace as you immerse yourself in the incredible beauty of the Universe.

December Intentions

Full Moon: December 14
New Moon: December 29

How will you consciously connect with nature this month?

TAKING ACTION!

What are the most important tasks you need to take action on to make progress this month?

The Monthly Forecast

Need a little guidance from the Universe?
Use your favourite tarot or oracle deck, and draw
three cards for December.

Opportunities　　　　　Challenges　　　　　Outcome

December: Rainbow Fluorite

Rainbow crystals symbolise boundless possibilities, as well as hope, joy, optimism, forgiveness, and fresh new beginnings. They remind us of the beauty that follows a devastating storm.

Take a rainbow fluorite (or any rainbow crystal) in one hand. Hold it tightly for a few minutes until you become aware of its vibrational energy.

As you hold the crystal, imagine yourself filled with the healing light of love. Ask yourself if there is anything you need to forgive yourself for. Imagine how the most powerful of cosmic energy works through the stone and into your hand, enabling you to the move into the future with a renewed sense of hope, peace and joy.

Thank the crystal for its powerful link to the Universe.

GRATITUDE LIST
What are you most grateful for in December?

1.
2.
3.
4.
5.
6.
7.
8.
9.
10.

Mandala Meditation

Interpretation

1. Notice the swirling waters of the ocean. The waves have their own divine beauty – they are changeless yet endlessly changing. Imagine how time dissolves into the vast ocean of all that is. Feel yourself entering into the waters. Imagine the ocean is within you and you are within the ocean. Relax into the endlessness of time and space.

2. Allow the cooling and soothing blue, green and purple colours of the water to harmonise in your mind and bring you peace and a deep sense of serenity. Consider the colours as shades of wisdom and spiritual self-fulfillment.

3. The fish symbolises the origin of things and the powers of rebirth. Think of the vastness of the ocean and absorb the harmony of the cosmos. As you draw the whole image of this mandala into

Soul Therapy

REFLECTIONS

What went well this month? What didn't go so well? What would you like to do differently next month?

A portion of the proceeds of the Soulwoman Life Planner will go to our charity, the David Sheldrick Wildlife Trust, a haven for elephant orphans, rhinos and other animals at risk.

SOULWOMANCIRCLES.COM

and so the Adventure BEGINS

Lightning Source UK Ltd.
Milton Keynes UK
UKOW07f1328040116

265748UK00008B/51/P